Colin and Fluffy Become Friends

Creator and illustrator: Patrick Arguin

English translation: Bleu Dactylo

French version written by: Michèle Rappe
Support, coaching and collaboration: Hélène Beaudette

I want to offer my deepest gratitude to Hélène Beaudette.
Her unconditional support and presence allowed TOOLS OF THE HEART to grow and come into form.

It's a beautiful and sunny day.
Colin, the oak, is swaying in the breeze when he notices
a little squirrel happily coming his way.

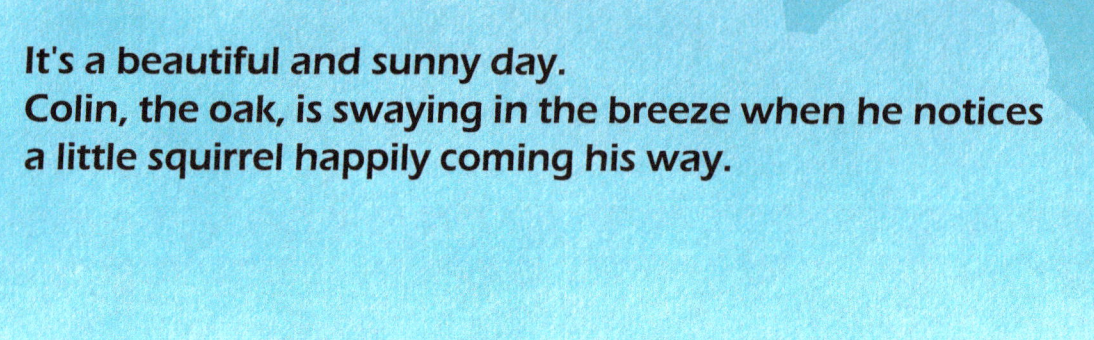

«Hello!» says the squirrel.
«My name is Fluffy! What is your name?»
The oak blushes a little and timidly replies,
«I'm Colin.»

Suddenly, an acorn falls to the ground
and Fluffy looks at it with desire.

«May I eat it?» he asks.
Colin hesitates but finally accepts.

Colin observes Fluffy enjoying himself.
«That squirrel seems really nice,» he thinks.

«That was delicious,» says Fluffy,
«thank you very much! Goodbye!»

The next day, Fluffy comes back to see Colin.
«Hello Colin, I'm happy to see you!»

«Hello Fluffy! I'm very happy to see you too.
Would you like to eat an acorn?»

«Oh! I would love to,» answers the squirrel.
«It's very nice of you.»

Fluffy enjoys his gift while telling one of his
many adventures in the garden.

As the days pass by, Colin and Fluffy get to know each other. The oak trusts him more and more and really enjoys Fluffy's friendship.

The playful squirrel enjoys climbing in the oak and jumping from branch to branch. How nice it is to have a friend!

One morning, Colin is worried. Fluffy did not come to visit him as he usually does.

Time passes by, and sadness fills Colin's heart. He wonders if Fluffy forgot about him.

«Maybe it's because I have no more acorns to offer him,» he thinks. He tells Mother Earth about his sadness.

«Dear Colin,» says Mother Earth with love, «even if you don't grow any acorns right now, you are still a wonderful and kind oak.»

«But Fluffy did not come to visit me,» he cries. «Maybe he doesn't like me anymore!»

«And you,» answers Mother Earth, «what do you think about yourself?» Colin is confused, he doesn't know what to say.

Father Sun overheard everything.
He proposes his help to Colin.
«To answer your question, you first need to
breathe in calmly. Inhale... Exhale...»

Colin closes his eyes and breathes in
deeply. He can feel the calm settling in him.

Guided by Father Sun, Colin goes into his heart and thinks about his beautiful rainbow of wisdom.

Green, the elf, appears and kindly approaches him.

«Your heart is like a treasure chest,» Green explains.
«It holds your joy, your kindness, and your self-confidence.
When the chest is open, love can shine brightly, and you
can feel it.»

«But sometimes, when you think you're not loved anymore
or when you are sad and disappointed, it is like you are
closing the lid and you may feel less love.»

Colin carefully listens to what the elf is saying. «You see Colin; you are the only one who can open or close your personal treasure chest.»

«This inner treasure is wonderful, and no one can ever take it away from you!»

«This treasure is YOU!»

Guided by Green, Colin imagines his heart opening wider and brighter than ever before.

A calming and peaceful green light hugs Colin.
There is a lot of love and warmth.

«Even when Fluffy is not around, your treasure is
always inside of you. So are the happy moments
that you have spent with him.»

Colin is happy!
He now understands that he can
feel good about himself, even when
he is alone.

«Knock! Knock!»
Colin opens his eyes and is pleasantly surprised to see Fluffy.
«Here I am,» says the squirrel. «I took a long stroll in the
garden today. I have tons of stories to tell you!»

«Me too!» says Colin. «But there is a cold wind now.
Would you like to come up and take shelter in my leaves?»

Fluffy comfortably nestles in the oak.
The two friends are having a great time
chatting and laughing together.

The Moon thinks of how friendship is
such a wonderful thing!

Remember...

How do we become friends with others?

To do that, you must dare to open your heart to others so they can get to know you better. For that, you will need to grow bigger than your fears, trust yourself, but also, trust others, even if you are shy or scared.

Is it normal to be scared at first?

When you meet someone for the first time, you don't know what they might think of you. It can sometimes seem scary. But the more you get to know each other, the more your friendship grows, and the fear slowly fades away.

What is a true friend?

A true friend is someone who appreciates you the way you are. They enjoy spending time with you and wish you good. If a conflict happens, it's important to explain to your friend how you feel and to listen to how they feel, so you can find a solution that will please you both.

The Book Collection

Tools of the Heart

Fostering Confidence and Self-esteem

1 Father Sun and Mother Earth Create Life
Breathing/Finding your rhythm

Breathing is essential to life; conscious breathing is a simple, yet effective way to regain your calm and well-being by finding your body's rhythm.

2 Fluffy and the Rainbow in his Heart
Meditation/Finding your inner calm

Each one of us has a peaceful place inside their heart. Meditation is a tool that allows you to find your personal space or to go back to it.

3 Colin Discovers Confidence
Grounding/Strengthening your self-confidence

Growing up often comes with its share of fears and hesitations. Growing solid roots helps to build and nurture a positive self-confidence.

4 Colin and Fluffy Become Friends
Knowing yourself/Loving and appreciating

Positive self-confidence and self-esteem are the building blocks of healthy relationships; therefore, learning to appreciate who we are is a treasure for life.

5 The Choice
Insight/Listening to your intuition

Learning to listen to your inner voice and how to trust it, is learning to stay true to yourself in all situations.

6 Colin's Courage
Expressing/Confidence in yourself

Standing up for yourself is not wrong. It is about relying on your self-worth with confidence, to respectfully say what you need to say.

7 Enough is Enough
Self-respect/Daring to be yourself

Developing good communication skills also implies expressing your feelings and needs in a respectful manner, which can sometimes be a challenge!

8 Fluffy Finds his Well-being
Self-awareness/Taking responsibility

Growing up is also about becoming more aware of your emotions and learning to manage them responsibly.

The Meditation Collection

Tools of the Heart

Fostering Confidence and Self-esteem

Specially designed for young children, the guided meditations explore and develop the same themes, as seen in the **Tools of the Heart** book collection. These intend to reinforce the children's knowledge of themselves through their inner space of wisdom, where things can be seen, heard, and felt.

Meditation is also a wonderful tool that children can easily learn to help them self-regulate physically, mentally, and emotionally.

To learn more, go to our website:

www.toolsoftheheart.com